T0063697

To: _____

From: _____

Date: _____

BEACH

Acknowledgments

To Bobbie Wilkinson, my twin sister and illustrator,
for her absolutely beautiful, original artwork and with thanks
for her constant love and laughter.

To my daughter, Kristin, of Adams Litke Design, Inc.,
for her beautiful design work in preparing the first draft of
this book and for her design contributions to the cover.
I am blessed to have you in my life.

To Dr. Paul Tingley of Paraclete Press for his friendship
and encouragement.

To Harvest House Publishers, for sharing my dream
and for your never-ending support. I am grateful to be part
of your incredible family.

Gentle Thoughts After Loss

Carol Hamblet Adams

Illustrated by Bobbie Wilkinson

HARVEST HOUSE PUBLISHERS
EUGENE, OREGON

Cover design by Studio Gearbox
Interior design by Chad Dougherty

Photo of Carol Hamblet Adams by Lydia Leclair Photography

For bulk, special sales, or ministry purchases, please call 1-800-547-8979.
Email: Customerservice@hhpbooks.com

This logo is a federally registered trademark of the Hawkins Children's LLC. Harvest House Publishers, Inc., is the exclusive licensee of this trademark.

Gentle Thoughts After Loss

Text copyright © 2024 by Carol Hamblet Adams
Artwork copyright © 2024 by Bobbie Wilkinson
Published by Harvest House Publishers
Eugene, Oregon 97408
www.harvesthousepublishers.com

ISBN 978-0-7369-8901-5 (hardcover)

Library of Congress Control Number: 2023946019

Printed in China

24 25 26 27 28 29 30 31 32 / RDS / 10 9 8 7 6 5 4 3 2 1

Dedication

To God, for blessing me so abundantly and for His inspiration and guidance on this project. To my incredibly special children, Kristin, Kevin, and Todd, who have always stood by me during good times as well as difficult times, and who supported both Steve and me with their faith, love, and constant encouragement during his illness. I am the luckiest mom in the world. To my children's spouses, Mike, Amanda, and Maura, and to my remarkable grandchildren, Rogers, Eamon, Oliver, Oscar, Stephen, and Stella, for adding so much joy to my life. I love you all.

*"My soul is weary with sorrow;
strengthen me according to your word."*

PSALM 119:28

My beloved husband, Steve, lived courageously with multiple sclerosis for most of our married life. He died from lymphoma shortly after our thirty-seventh wedding anniversary. I can see now how Jesus was with me every step of the way. Through the darkest of times, Jesus stood patiently by—comforting me, supporting me, and surrounding me with His grace and His love.

After Steve died, I read every book on grief that I could find. Oftentimes, the books were long and difficult to read. I needed a book that was very simple and easy to understand. I needed gentle, peaceful, encouraging words to help me find hope again.

And so I have written *Gentle Thoughts After Loss*—thoughts that have taken me years to learn myself; thoughts I still need to read and reread.

Maybe your loss was a loved one, your health, your job, your security, your freedom, or your spirit. Whatever it was, I promise Jesus is right there with you today, holding your hand and seeing you through.

May these simple words bring peace and comfort to you in some small way and help you know you are not alone.

Please be assured of my deepest prayers as you journey through your loss.

Blessings and love,

Carol

I will get
through this with
God's help.

No matter what happens to me today,
God is with me and will help see me through.
I am not alone.

*"Do not be afraid; do not be discouraged, for the
Lord your God will be with you wherever you go."*

JOSHUA 1:9

I will be gentle
with myself.

I will only do what I am comfortable doing and what I have the energy for.

"Take My yoke upon you and learn from Me, for I am gentle and humble in heart, and you will find rest for your souls."

MATTHEW 11:29 NKJV

I am stronger
than I think.

I thank God for the great strength it takes to simply be, even when I hurt so deeply there seems to be nothing left of me.

"I can do all this through him who gives me strength."

PHILIPPIANS 4:13

I will make
major decisions
later.

In time, with God's help,
I will know what to do and when.

"Show me Your ways, O LORD, teach me Your paths."

PSALM 25:4 NKJV

I will
just keep
breathing.

When I get overwhelmed, I will focus on my breathing. Deep breaths in and out. That's enough for today.

"The Spirit of God has made me, and the breath of the Almighty gives me life."

JOB 33:4 ESV

I will feel
my feelings.

May I be strong enough to feel my every emotion. That is how I will get through.

"God is our refuge and strength,
a very present help in trouble."

PSALM 46:1 ESV

I will
accept my
feelings.

My feelings are all valid. They are neither right nor wrong. May I always accept my feelings in order to heal.

"To everything there is a season, a time for every purpose under heaven...a time to weep, and a time to laugh; a time to mourn, and a time to dance."

ECCLESIASTES 3:1, 4 NKJV

It's okay
not to be okay.

If I'm feeling afraid, alone, angry, sad, discouraged, lost or empty, that's okay. I need to give myself permission to be human.

"The Lord is close to the brokenhearted and those who are crushed in spirit He saves."

PSALM 34:18

I will let my tears flow.

Tears show how deeply we have loved.
They wash us clean and help us begin again.

*"I have heard your prayer and seen
your tears; I will heal you."*

2 KINGS 20:5

I will tell God
what I need.

Our heavenly Father wants us to come to Him and share our every need. He will always be there to support us.

"Do not be anxious about anything, but in everything by prayer and supplication with thanksgiving let your requests be made known to God."

PHILIPPIANS 4:6 ESV

I will ask
for help when
I need it.

When my heart gets too heavy, I will ask for
help and remember that seeking support is
a sign of strength, not weakness.

*"Come to me, all you who are weary and
burdened, and I will give you rest."*

MATTHEW 11:28

I will lean on
my family
and friends.

I am grateful for my family and friends who care. I will lean on them when I need to and let them know when I need to be alone.

"Love one another as I have loved you."

JOHN 15:12 CSB

I will lovingly
take care
of myself.

I will nurture myself physically, mentally,
and spiritually, with love and compassion.

"This will bring health to your body."

PROVERBS 3:8

I will remember that a special occasion is just another day.

If I am unable to join others for a holiday or special occasion, that's okay. If others don't understand, that's okay too.

"Yet I am not alone, for my Father is with me."

JOHN 16:32

It's okay
not to
believe.

Others are lifting me up in prayer when I'm unable to pray. God understands and loves me unconditionally.

"Lord, I believe; help my unbelief!"

MARK 9:24 NKJV

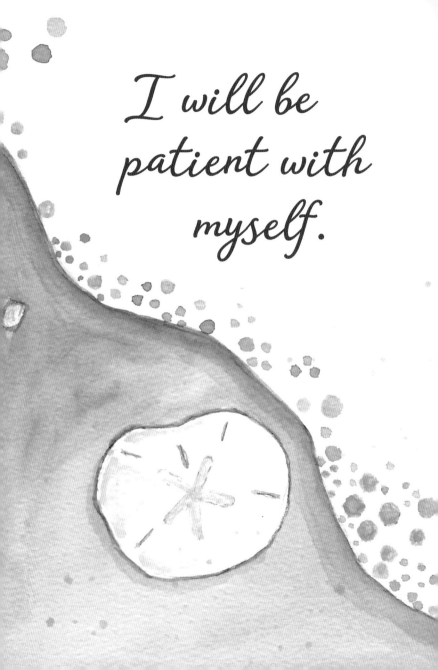

I will be
patient with
myself.

There is no timetable for grief. I will be kind to myself and will heal at my own pace.

"You will be strengthened with all his glorious power, so you will have all the endurance and patience you need."

COLOSSIANS 1:11 NLT

I will be patient with God.

I often get impatient waiting for my prayers to be answered. May I remember God's timing is always better than mine.

"I waited patiently for the LORD; he turned to me and heard my cry."

PSALM 40:1

I will try to
keep life simple.

Less is always more. I will make room for what matters most to me.

"The LORD is my shepherd; I shall not want."

PSALM 23:1 ESV

It's okay
to do nothing.

It's good to take "time-outs" from life.
That's how I will refresh myself.

*"I will personally go with you...
and I will give you rest."*

EXODUS 33:14 NLT

I will keep joy
and fun in my life.

Children teach us so much about living life with joy. I will awaken the child within me.

"A cheerful heart is good medicine."

PROVERBS 17:22

I will forgive myself.

Guilt keeps me from healing.
I will choose to forgive myself and
go forward with a clean heart.

"He is faithful and just and will forgive us our sins."

1 JOHN 1:9

I will
forgive others.

Peace comes from forgiveness. May I always remember people are doing the best they can.

"If you forgive those who sin against you, your heavenly Father will forgive you."

MATTHEW 6:14 NLT

I will love myself unconditionally.

I will try to love myself and remember that, in my brokenness, I am still whole and complete in God's sight.

"For you created my inmost being; you knit me together in my mother's womb. I praise you because I am fearfully and wonderfully made."

PSALM 139:13-14

I will try
to be still.

In silence and in stillness,
there is great healing.

"Be still, and know that I am God."

PSALM 46:10

I will try not to
have any regrets.

May I be comforted knowing I have always done my best at any given moment.

"Forget the former things; do not dwell on the past."

ISAIAH 43:18

I will never give up.

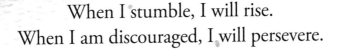

When I stumble, I will rise.
When I am discouraged, I will persevere.

*"Be strong and do not give up, for
your work will be rewarded."*

2 CHRONICLES 15:7

I will try to
help others.

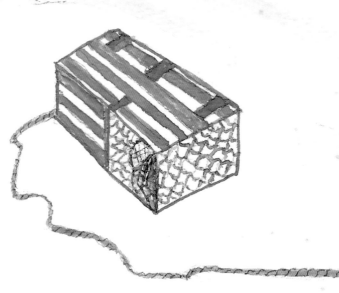

When I am able to, I will reach out to others.
Every small gift of kindness will help
my heart mend.

*"Truly I tell you, whatever you did for one of the least
of these brothers and sisters of mine, you did for me."*

MATTHEW 25:40

I am thankful
for my faith.

I am grateful for the precious gift of faith that keeps me strong when I am weak, that keeps me going when it would be easier to quit.

"Continue to live your lives in him…strengthened in the faith as you were taught, and overflowing with thankfulness."

COLOSSIANS 2:6-7

I will practice
faith over fear.

It's easy to allow fear to overtake me.
If I give God my burdens, He will take them
and give me His peace.

*"For I, the L*ORD *your God, will hold your right
hand, saying to you, 'Fear not, I will help you.'"*

ISAIAH 41:13 NKJV

I will try not
to expect things
from others.

I will appreciate those who can be there for me and pray for those who can't.

"Do good, and lend, expecting nothing in return, and your reward will be great."

LUKE 6:35 ESV

I will live one
day at a time.

And if that's too much,
I will live one moment at a time.

"Don't be anxious about tomorrow. God will take care of your tomorrow too. Live one day at a time."

MATTHEW 6:34 TLB

I will set
new goals.

I'll begin by just getting through today.
In time, I will set new goals to help lift
my spirits and give me hope.

"'For I know the plans I have for you,' declares the
Lord…'plans to give you hope and a future.'"

JEREMIAH 29:11

I will honor my memories.

In time, sad memories will be replaced with happy ones. I will honor these cherished memories and keep them alive in my heart all the days of my life.

"The righteous one will be remembered forever."

PSALM 112:6 CSB

My loved one
is still close.

When loved ones die, they still remain by
our sides to comfort, guide, and love us
until we are together again.

*"Now is your time of grief, but I will see you again and
you will rejoice, and no one will take away your joy."*

JOHN 16:22

I am brave.

May I have the strength to begin each day
by putting one foot in front of the other.

"When I am afraid, I put my trust in
you. In God, whose word I praise."

PSALM 56:3-4

I am courageous.

It takes courage to get through
each day. If no one is around
to tell me "Good job!" then
I will tell myself.

"Take courage! It is I. Don't be afraid."

MATTHEW 14:27

I am grateful.

I thank God for all my blessings. Gratitude helps me see beauty and love all around.

*"Give thanks to the L*ORD*, for he is good; his love endures forever."*

1 CHRONICLES 16:34

I believe the sun
will shine again.

In my brokenness, I believe the sun will shine through the darkness.

"God's love and kindness will shine upon us like the sun that rises in the sky."

LUKE 1:78 CEV

I believe in myself.

I am worthy of all my hopes and dreams.

"You are precious and honored in my sight."

ISAIAH 43:4

I will hope again.

With God, there is always hope for today
and hope for tomorrow.

*"Those who hope in the LORD will renew their strength.
They will soar on wings like eagles; they will run and
not grow weary, they will walk and not be faint."*

ISAIAH 40:31

I will trust again.

May I have faith enough to trust God
is guiding my life every day.

*"Trust in the L*ORD *with all your heart and
lean not on your own understanding."*

PROVERBS 3:5

I will dream again.

It's never too late to dream or to believe in
the magic of your dreams coming true.

*"May he grant you your heart's desire
and fulfill all your plans!"*

PSALM 20:4 ESV

I am at peace.

When I give God my anxiety, my pain,
my doubts and my fears,
He will give me His peace.

"Peace I leave with you; my peace I give you…
Do not let your hearts be troubled and do not be afraid."

JOHN 14:27

I believe...

In God
In life
In love
In myself
In my dreams
In new beginnings
In today
In tomorrow

*"I tell you, whatever you ask for in prayer, believe
that you have received it, and it will be yours."*

MARK 11:24

I will begin my
new journey now.

The rest of my life begins today.

"He leads me beside still waters.
He restores my soul."

PSALM 23:2-3 ESV

Meet the Author

Carol Hamblet Adams is a motivational speaker and the author of six books, including *My Beautiful Broken Shell: Words of Hope to Refresh the Soul.* She has spent many years in the grief ministry. Carol's life centers around her faith, her family, her friends, and God's magnificent seashore. She is the proud mom of three children and the proud gramma of six grandchildren. Carol can be reached on the beach or at carolhambletadams@comcast.net.

About the Illustrator

Bobbie Wilkinson is a Christian writer, artist, and musician. She is the proud mother of three daughters—Robyn, Kelly, and Brooke—and the lucky gramma of five grandchildren—Ada, Owen, Hoyt, Frankie, and Wren. She and her husband, Tom, along with their adored little dog, Shelly, live in a self-renovated barn in the northern Virginia countryside. When Bobbie grows up, she wants to live in a small cottage by the sea. She can be reached at bobbiewilkinson1@gmail.com.